THE FINAL CHAPTER...

Understanding the Journey

PAMELA K. MILLS

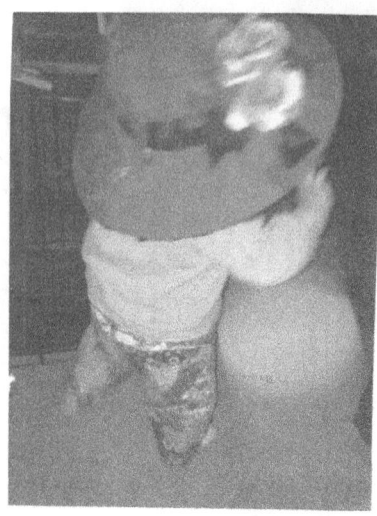

This photo was taken in the living room of Pamela Mills. The small orb shows that past loved ones are with us even if they are not in the "form" that we can see with our normal vision.

CONTENTS

Acknowledgments	v
1. We are only given a glimpse ...	1
Protections	2
2. We are Heavenly Creatures having an Earthly Experience	18
Our Earthly Experience	19
3. Universal Designation as an Evolving Entity	23
Universal Designation	24
4. Atonement	28
Atonement	29
5. Processing and the Journey	33
Processing and the Journey	34
6. End of Life Processes	41
What does the body experience at the end of life?	42
7. No one transitions from this life to the next alone	47
Those who have gone before will assist with my transition	48
8. "In the Beginning ....."	64
The beginning	65
Thoughts from the Author	87
Call to Action	89

ACKNOWLEDGMENTS

I would like to thank all the Hospice Staff that I have worked with over the years.

St Francis Home Health and Hospice in Litchfield IL, and Acclaim Hospice in Dayton Ohio. The management team members of Kathy Schwab RN in Litchfield IL, as well as Jim Venelle and Cindy Henderson RN in Dayton OH, who provided me with the autonomy to seek information and work with the families and Hospice patients as they took this journey. They understood both the need to allow the family to go through this but also recognized the fact that it was new to most of them, and they needed a guide to reassure them and assist in paving the path forward.

A thank you to the management staff that allowed me to spend the time needed to work through the issues with which the individuals were dealing at the end of life. Also, a huge thank you to the nurses, aides and ministerial staff that provided the intimate and spiritual care that the individuals required.

A huge thank you to the families that allowed me to become a part of their lives during this personal time of transition.

Finally, a thank you to the family and friends that helped with this project by reading, critiquing, and keeping me on track with ideas thoughts and photos!

Forever Grateful!

Pamela

The Cover Photo was taken by Renee Arnold and she graciously has allowed me to use it for this book. She also edited this book and provided me with great feedback.

Copyright © 2021 **by Pamela K Mills** LISW-S ACHt SAP

"The Final Chapter...Understanding the Journey" is book one of a series of books discussing the various stages of life and the lessons that are learned as we participate in life.

All rights reserved. No part of this publication may be reproduced, distributed, or transmitted in any form or by any means, including photocopying, recording, or other electronic or mechanical methods, without the prior written permission of the publisher, except in the case of brief quotations embodied in critical reviews, and certain other noncommercial uses permitted by copyright law.

Although the author and publisher have made every effort to ensure that the information in this book was correct at press time, the author and publisher do not assume and hereby disclaim any liability to any party for any loss, damage, or disruption caused by errors or omissions, whether such errors or omissions result from negligence, accident, or any other cause. Adherence to all applicable laws and regulations, including international, federal, state, and local governing professional licensing, business practices, advertising, and all other aspects of doing business in the US, Canada or any other jurisdiction is the sole responsibility of the reader and consumer.

Neither the author nor the publisher assumes any responsibility or liability whatsoever on behalf of the consumer or reader of this material. Any perceived slight of any individual or organization is purely unintentional. The resources in this book are provided for informational purposes only and should not be used to replace the specialized training and professional judgment of a health care or mental health care professional. Neither the author nor the publisher can be held responsible for the use of the information provided within this book. Please always consult a trained professional before making any decision regarding treatment of yourself or others.

This book is dedicated to:
My Mother, Donna Jean Watson, and my Father Joe Crabill. They provided me with the interest in things that are not part of the normal experience and the courage to explore those very things without judging or diminishing them in any way.

Also, to by siblings, Lonna Crabill Nelson, Kimberly Crabill Bowers, Joseph Crabill and Jeffery Crabill. They were the best siblings ever though all the trials and episodes that we experienced in our lives. They also enjoy the areas of interest that I am bringing forth both in this book and subsequent books that will be written and published.

PROLOGUE

As we go through life we mature physically and emotionally. We transition through all the various stages in life starting with infancy -> childhood -> adolescence -> teenager -> young adulthood -> middle age -> senior citizen and finally we transition to the next level of existence.

The following narratives are not written as the "be all end all" of the life transitioning process, but they are meant to provide the reader with a starting place. You can use the information to provide a starting point that allows you to understand what your loved ones, or those we care for at end of life, are experiencing.

You will be able to begin interpreting and understanding a small part of the process that is involved with transitioning from this life to the next level, as it is experienced by those mentioned in these writings.

Your loved one may not experience all of the different situations but be open to what they are experiencing and ask questions. They want to share with you, and this is a perfect time to allow them to share.

I
WE ARE ONLY GIVEN A GLIMPSE
...

"If you are speaking you are missing the chance to listen and learn."

PROTECTIONS

We are only given a glimpse of what occurs or what to expect through the perspective of those who are transitioning but that glimpse allows us, as the caregiver, to respect and provide them with the peace and acceptance needed.

As I learned more about the end-of-life process, I wanted to ask questions and paid close attention to what they were sharing with me. They were willing to share their experiences and I wanted to share that knowledge with others so they could use this insight to the advantage of those transitioning. I listened and allowed those immersed in the end-of-life process to tell me what was occurring. I listened without judgement and they corrected my interpretation when needed.

It is important to understand that there is a partition, I will call it the Veil, that separates the different levels of existence. The Bible refers to those that transition to the other side of the Veil as spirits or souls. These souls consist of the energy that we possess that allows us to use the physical body as we go through life.

I believe that this Veil exists to "protect" us from our

brain being inundated with situations that it cannot handle or explain. The primary goal of the brain is to make order of information. We would be overwhelmed if we not only perceived of the lives and situations on this side of the Veil but also had to filter the things that are occurring on the other side of the Veil. We are sent to learn and teach lessons so that we can move to the next level of existence, and we need to be able to focus on those lessons.

The people that I speak of in this writing are those that I specifically sat with as they were transitioning. Some I spent a year with, and they allowed me to take that journey with them as far as they could, others I may have only been with a few hours, but I was able to assist them to understand what was happening. We shared many experiences and I was able to interact with their family members both living and those who had crossed over.

As people are working through the end-of-life challenges, they no longer have any vested interest in stating things nicely. They say what they mean and allow you to react and work from there. They become brutally honest and that may be difficult at times, but it also allows you to ask questions about what they are seeing and experiencing, and they will answer knowing that you are not afraid of what is happening. They are not mean about what they tell you but often they forget that you cannot see what they are experiencing, and they may become frustrated.

One of my transitioning friends told me that we, the "living", are not able to understand the entire process because we have no words in our language to describe the beauty of what they have seen.

Time frames morph and take on a different aspect as we transition. They may sleep long periods but when they awaken it seems to them to have only been a few minutes. They mentally jump from current times to long past times and may not understand why you cannot follow their story. When you try to talk to them about today, yesterday, or tomorrow they do not follow due to the time frame issue. It is better to talk with them about the occurrence or occasion so that they have a concrete idea of what you are talking or speaking about. They have a grasp of occurrence just not an understanding of something that happened in 2015.

The look of peace that sweeps across their face and the relaxation that the body displays as they experience this transition provides others with a sense of comfort related to their passing because as we see it "they are not suffering".

As humans we equate death and dying with suffering. If someone groans it is assumed that it is because they are suffering. In the reality of the transitioning world, it may be a groan because they are meeting someone they have not known in this life or an experience that they had in the past that they are working through and atoning for prior to the final transition.

Historically our family provided care in the home as we were going into the end-of-life situations. The elderly provided child care if the parents had to leave the home for a period of time, they provided the wisdom needed to farm and raise livestock, and assisted with the household chores. When we became ill at end of life we were comforted and cared for in the home. If the doctor was needed they would come to the home and provide care in the home. When the loved one passed they were cleaned and dressed in the home and literally laid out on the dinning room table. The wake was held there and all the family and friends in the community would come to the home to pay their respects. That allowed all generations to understand and deal with the life stages from birth to end-of-life. Individuals understood the life process and held them sacred even though parts of them were painful.

In the last 50 years we have institutionalized the process of death. We have nursing homes to provide care to our loved ones who are living longer. Families use the excuses of not being available or not understanding nursing processes. We no longer experience the aging process in a close-up and personal situation.

Nursing homes send their residents to the hospital when they know that death is imminent. There are several reasons for this action, one is the nursing home can show that no one dies in their care, statistics are important in long term care. Another reason is because if that person passes peacefully in the nursing home the family can sue the facility because they say the staff did not pay attention and their loved one died not receiving appropriate care. Whether the patient did or did not get the care needed the facility settles with the family to save a court trial that can get very expensive. We have removed from our loved ones the right to pass peacefully in an environment that they know to avoid litigation.

Hospice has given the patient the right to pass peacefully and stay in an environment in which they are comfortable, and it allows them to teach those caring for them the end-of-life lessons that are important for us to know about life transitioning.

They teach us with loving understanding that transitioning to the next level is not something to be feared but something to be embraced and it should occupy a special place in our heart and our lives. It also teaches us that life does not end with the body dying but it is a transition to the next level of existence. We do not just live and then die to be buried or cremated. We live a life learning or teaching lessons so that we can move to the next level of existence well prepared for the next "life" ahead of us.

As we take on the challenges of living, we encounter a variety of situations that allow us to see more clearly who we are and what our purpose during this earthly experience entails. We may go into a situation fearful but as we emerge from that learning situation, we come out stronger and more grounded.

Life situations may include childhood challenges, high school growth and development and the transitioning into young adulthood. Those areas lead to the next area of life that includes marriage, family, losses, and parenthood.

Each of these situations provides more lessons that allow us to grow and learn many of the lessons that we need to complete our life journey. These lessons include letting go of our ego, our need to control others and the fear that is part of learning. We learn that when our ego gets in the front of the line in our life priorities, we are not able to process or understand what others may need from us to move forward in their lives.

Often, we forget that most scholars and spiritual teachers stress the importance of letting go of the ego and allowing the heart to lead. By allowing others to take the place of ourselves in life we are able to learn from their prospective and understand the universe in another small way. There is so much to learn in life that we need to take every opportunity to absorb and process the lessons that are available.

Several lessons that we learn are relationship bound. Things like jealousy, sharing, loving on multiple levels and spiritual growth. They are all intertwined but each is a lesson that will stand on its own.

Love vs Jealousy are two lessons that we must realize are joined together. As children, if we are raised in a home that is based on pitting one child against the other for affection, or a home that feels it is alright to molest or use a child for what they can do for us as the parents, as opposed to raising our children in a loving home allowing them to become the amazing God blessing that they are, we not only multiply the lessons that we must learn but we also multiply the lessons that our children must now learn.

I have worked with many adults who hate not only themselves, their parents but their entire lives. They were forced to deal with the inability to love themselves and those around them. Their children carry on the traditions as they are passed through the family. This is a cycle that carries on and moves through generations.

Another theory is that our DNA may be impacted by situations that may have frightened or injured someone in a past generation. This event nicked the

DNA because it was so impactful and traumatizing and this nick is then transferred via the DNA to future generations. As this is passed down certain fears are transferred, and we possess that fear through no fault of our own.

It is important that we learn what our fears are and how they occurred. Personally, I had a fear of the dark, a fear of being stabbed in the back while sleeping and a fear of fire. The fear of being stabbed was pervasive from the age of about 3. I would sleep with my bed next to the wall, my back on the wall and my feet under the blankets, even when it was 100 degrees. It was crazy, I had never been stabbed and never watched a movie that had a stabbing. I was so young I could not have had this as a memory.

While contemplating this I was aware that I had a family history of Native American heritage and began exploring this area. I am a practicing hypnotherapist and worked with others to do a regression. At that point it appeared that a family member may have been stabbed and this may be the nick origination. The Indian tradition was to ceremonially cremate their dead so this may have been another nick on the DNA. After recognizing those things, I no longer have the fear of being stabbed while sleeping nor do I fear fire. If you are going to work on these types of issues, please make sure that you are working with a reputable hypnotist who has undergone extensive training. Your fears do not necessarily mean that you have a nicked DNA it may be more related to issues from your childhood.

While many updates and new ideas are coming forth as they relate to end-of-life there are still so many things that we do not know. Recently they are looking into the fact that the brain cells live approximately 4 days after the rest of the body cells die from lack of oxygen.

BASIC INFORMATION REQUIRED TO ASSIST OTHERS:

As you are working with individuals at the end of life it is important to understand what their life was like. Was it a loving family, a stress related relationship with the spouse and/or children, a situation that was lacking in the basic needs?

Their religious perspective is also important. Not in the aspect of how often they attended church but instead the strength of their belief system and the place that it took in their daily lives. If they were a religious person and were often in prayer you will need to begin your journey with them understanding what the position God played in their lives. Each religion has a specific teaching about what is approved or not approved with others interacting with the dying.

Respect requires a basic understanding not only of that but also an understanding of how to interact with them.

I was working with an African American woman at end of life, and she sang at the top of her lungs through most of the process. She enjoyed the singing, and she was praising God as she had learned through life. She was without her family at this particular time since they were traveling but we were all able to join in her songs as she was passing. She spread a gesture of love and spirituality until she passed.

Not all individuals that are passing are open to sharing and you also must allow that to be part of the process. Those who are quiet may be working on the part of forgiveness and atonement. This is very important and is another process that must be completed on a personal basis. We cannot intrude on others as they work through the processes. It is always important to allow them the space needed to complete their journey.

When you feel that the person you are working with is in distress, either by what they have shared with you or what you intuitively pick up from that person you must allow them to make their own choices. You can not force or guide them into a solution that works for you, it is not the solution that they need and this may only prolong their process.

I have worked with many people as they were

passing and I have only met 3 who were looking at hell, or some sort of very negative outcome. These individuals were frightened, fought to get away from something that appeared to be pursuing them, and had an extended end of life process.

Each of them had family that reported that they were extremely difficult to deal with throughout life. They were controlling and hostile to them, jealous of the others that came into their children's lives and tried multiple methods of breaking the new family's life. These are issues that not only the person who is now transitioning must reconcile and atone for, but it now passes the guilt and anxiety down to the new generation to deal with and resolve.

These are not issues related to spirituality or religion, they are issues related to how the ego gets in the way of loving others and allowing them to follow their own path through life. Control and demanding of loyalty and dominance are the root of these issues. If they refuse to atone or forgive themselves or others, they move that issue forward during their transition. They have not learned the lessons that they were sent to learn during this life.

Perhaps the literal view of hell may be the result of not learning what was attempted in this life and the lessons of the next level carry a higher physical impact to get their attention. Because the sense of time is no longer relevant after the transition our understanding of hell is an eternity.

Those that I worked with showed a definite understanding of where they were transitioning to, and they fought as long as they could to stay here. They could see what was ahead and did not want to go there.

They also seemed to have an understanding of what should be done to correct or change their destination and they actively chose not to follow that path.

One person that I was with was reacting to my visit in an unusual manner. She was actively transitioning and each time she would reach out to me and touch my hand she would scream as loud as she could until she let go. Then we would carry on a conversation as we did before. Then she would reach out for my hand again and scream again and this continued. Even with my history of experience this was the first time that I had ever experienced this. I knew intuitively that she was aware of what her journey required at this time. I suggested that she knew what she needed to do and she looked at me with a very hardened look and said "no". She refused to do what her journey required and fought her transitioning as long as she had the physical strength to continue. It is important to note that she reached for my hand each time, I did not make any attempt to touch her. It appeared that she may have thought I could have provided some type of intervention. As an observer there is nothing that you can do to intervene. You must allow the sojourner the right and privilege to take their own path. You are not there to set their course for them because to do that takes from them the right to learn the lessons needed.

I could tell from her look that the place she was transitioning to was not a place that I would want to go, but it was a place that she was going because her ego would not allow her to put it aside and move forward with forgiving herself or others.

After finishing my work with this family, a daughter that I had been in contact with called to get information on a grief support group in her area. I had been told by the father that she lived in St Louis MO. When I talked to her, she requested that I not tell her father where she lived, that all 5 of the children had kept that information from them due to the fact that their mother was so hateful and their father never stepped in to assist them or stop her.

She actually lived in California with her brother, her other brother told them he lived in Michigan and he actually lived in Florida and there was another brother that never spoke with them again after he left home. When he came home in the summers from the military school, they had all been shipped to from the age of 5 years, he would clear out the shed behind the house and live there. What a horrific situation that they were placed in without any person speaking out for them or making any attempt to assist them.

They felt that they could not let either of the parents know where they lived out of fear of reprisal and the fear of them seeking out their home which was now their safety.

I would often try to reunite families and make attempts to find at least one area they could communicate with the person that was transitioning. One son who was raised in a similar situation to the above family would come to see his mother but was often leaving in tears. Even as an adult who was transitioning, she withheld the love and acceptance that the child needed.

It was, at this point in time, a deliberate and hateful act. These acts now pile on to their children another lesson to learn about forgiving those who would not ask and would not forgive others. It is difficult to forgive those filled with hate but often that is the very person that our lessons are wrapped around. Hate is an all-encompassing emotion that takes a lot of energy to maintain and a great deal of peace to let go. We can not move forward with transitioning until the hate that we experienced as physically living entities is resolved and let go.

Moving on to a more pleasant time of transitioning, what the person experiences is often a part of what their life history has involved. As I worked with people. I learned that each story is unique but has the same grounding in the process. You will be able to see that as you read the stories in the later part of this book.

One question that I liked to ask those who are transitioning, is to think of one of the most pleasant days that you can remember. What was the setting, who was there, what importance did they play in your life?

Was it sunny, warm, peaceful? What adjectives would you use to describe this? We have several days that are based on just snippets of what our entire life involved. We should wrap our arms around the positive and peaceful emotions and allow the negative to go. Give them wings to leave and not take them back. One of the most difficult things to do is to allow the peace of the world to come in and take the place of the negatives that we have used throughout life to define and identify us as a person. We are not the negatives; we are the positive things that we have provided to those around us and the encouragement that others have received from us.

Often our view of ourselves is different than the view that others have of us as individuals. In my next book, I intend to work with the reader to not only accept who we are but also the lessons to be learned so we can use our energy to depart onto others the positive lessons that the universe has to enjoy. That book will be

Whispering Universe, Understanding the Journey to be released in fall of 2021.

Learning to listen and share our experiences with others allows us to touch base with like minded individuals who are also on this journey. It is a self-effacing trek that we adapt and encourage others to seek their own understanding as we move forward.

Human Beings are wired to question and learn, changing and adapting things as they work through the challenges that life provides. I can not stress enough that life is about learning and teaching.

2
WE ARE HEAVENLY CREATURES HAVING AN EARTHLY EXPERIENCE

Are you the person that you think you are, or is there more to you than just the side that you see each day?

OUR EARTHLY EXPERIENCE

It is not difficult to realize that as we go through life we are always learning or teaching lessons. We may not think of ourselves as teachers but every day we are learning and teaching. Children react with stunned amazement as they learn how the world works and we, as adults, should allow ourselves the grace to embrace the lessons and rejoice in the learning.

We may make colossal mistakes and we must learn to take those in stride along with the amazing positive things that we are able to do for ourselves and others. The lessons may not be attached to major learning events but to the mundane things that provide us with the survival skills that are needed in daily situations.

Every day we have lessons teaching us to avoid situations, to use our skills to our advantage, that kindness in any form outweighs the negative things that occur when we are cruel to others and the coping skills needed to survive. There are many cliches that people use to assist themselves to get through situations. They include "life is short take a chance", "The only bad decision is no decision", and one of my favorites is "suck it up butter cup". Each works to attach itself to our positive self-worth allowing us to start the learning lessons from a strong positive position.

One belief system is that once we are finished teaching and learning our life lessons, we can leave the body and return to our heavenly home. Put simply that philosophy is that *we are heavenly creatures having an earthly experience.*

One person shared with me that she was able to see her entire life as a tapestry, it was more beautiful than she realized. Every detail was there, and she was able to understand why all the things she saw as "bad" as she was experiencing them had to happen so that all the "good" and beautiful things could follow in the natural order they were intended to occur.

How can we know hope if we have never experienced despair? Bad happens and the good can follow.

Bethel was extremely poor, had worked hard her entire life but never seemed to get ahead financially or socially. What she had not recognized was that she had emotionally affected every person that she encountered, and she was a positive and happy person. Without a doubt most of those people were with her at the end of her life, she was always happy and would talk of those that she had been able to see again during this process.

How we use those lessons and move forward is based on a variety of things that many assume are out of our control. My belief is that most things are within our control and how we handle those situations determines the path that our life may take. As Robert Frost wrote "two paths diverged into a woods, and I took the one less traveled by, and that has made all the difference".

I personally embrace the philosophy *that we are heavenly creatures having an earthly experience*. We are placed in this life at a specific time, with the others around us to learn the lessons that all are teaching. At the same time, we help them learn the lessons that they are here to learn. It is a process, an evolution of experience.

Whether you decide that God is an entity or that nature is the higher power, you must understand that the energy that moves us throughout the day is the energy that is released back into that higher power at end of life, "energy is neither created nor destroyed, it simply changes form", which Julius Robert Mayor determined to be the conservation of energy in 1842. That theory is now referred to as the Law of Thermodynamics.

I have had the privilege of working with hundreds of people that were either in Hospice formally or were in the last stages of life and I provided services through a home health program or privately provided mental health services.

Each person has a unique story that is based on

their life and their personal journey. My most cherished memories are of the experiences that they shared as they moved from this physical life to the next level of existence. Every story was different and very emotionally intense to those involved.

The amazing thing is that I have a seat at their side learning and assisting in their life lessons so that the transition can be easier and the lessons can be learned by all involved.

Each persons' lessons are not only something that they can learn from, but it is also something that others involved in their life can learn and not need to relearn later.

3

UNIVERSAL DESIGNATION AS AN EVOLVING ENTITY

They knew I was coming and appeared to know me, but we had never met.

UNIVERSAL DESIGNATION AS AN EVOLVING ENTITY

One interesting thing is that those in the process of transitioning all appeared to know me. I had never met them prior to seeing them at the end of their lives, but they spoke to me as a person that was meant to be there.

They knew I was coming, and one individual told me she had been waiting on me to arrive and was so glad I finally got there. I introduced myself to her and told her my name was Pam. She looked at me intently and said clearly, "that is not the name I know you by". Before I could ask her "what name" she knew me by, she passed very peacefully holding my hand. The question that I carry to this day is are we known in different realms by different monikers, by which others identify our energy or spirit? Do we eventually know what those names are?

As an observer you provide that person with a vessel to share their experience and you are able learn from what they express. As the vessel it is my assumption that you become what they need to speak their truth.

They long to share the amazing things that are occurring as they wait for the next level of existence to envelop them permanently in its warm embrace. This may be the last lesson that they are to teach, and one of the many that you have yet to learn.

As you walk with someone during this time you learn that they are a spiritual energy. As humans we identify others by not only physical characteristics but also by those social yokes that we walk with daily that identify the roles that we take on in life. Husband, wife, child, teacher, social worker, and many other titles that help to identify us in this life, on this side of the Veil. Each identifier teaches a lesson that we will carry forward into the next level of existence.

Others come to know us by those monikers, they can generalize what a typical person with that moniker does and they can transfer that information to us and have a better understanding of what our roles are as a person or actor in this life.

The universal question then becomes do we drop those monikers in the next level of existence or do we maintain them. As those I worked with see their loved ones in the transitioning time they know them by the names that were used here in this life time but they also appear to understand what their role was during this time. Husband, wife, daughter and so on. When I would ask who was with us, they were able to identify them according to their relationship to them in this life.

Bethel was able to identify the two adults and two

children who kept coming to her in her "dreams" later in the process as her two cousins and their children who crossed over during the depression. She did not identify them by name but she knew who they were and what happened to them and how specifically how they were related to her in this life time.

Others were able to tell me who they were with, but they did not always call them by name, they were aware of how they were related to them. One example is the individual who saw the man at the foot of the bed, and as he moved closer, she was aware of who he was and his importance to her but did not identify him by name, only by his social role and how he related to her. It was her husband dressed in a tuxedo because it would be their 50th wedding anniversary.

Spiritual guides do not go into detail as to whether we will or will not know those we have interacted with in this life as we transition to the next level. They speak only of the lessons that we must learn to move on a provide a glimpse of the lessons and egoless existence that is required.

Some of the lessons are passed on through whisperings that are quiet and move us to find our "true selves" and what we as independent individuals believe. Things that are our truth and the truths we live by. We must learn what our reality entails and move forward with things.

Each of the individuals that I was privileged to sit with during this time was able to identify their truth and know that they had learned the lessons they needed to learn.

4
ATONEMENT

We all must atone for the things that we have done to others as well as for the things that we feel we may have done or should have done.

ATONEMENT

One interesting factor is that regardless of the physical condition that the person is experiencing such as, bedfast and unable to move or still able to get up and about on a limited basis, they all were very cognitively active. As you watch the expressions on their faces move easily from smiling to expressions of concern or even frowns at times, they are working through all the things that have happened to them during their time on earth. Some things were of their own doing while other things happened to them. All must be accounted for and resolved.

I was making two visits weekly to Bethel as she transitioned. As I had mentioned previously Bethel was very poor financially but very rich spiritually as she had shared her life and done for others in every way she was able to share.

Bethel was in a lot of pain and was bed fast. She required others to assist her even to reposition in the bed. This made her dependent on others for everything from moving, changing her soiled clothing, feeding her, as well as giving her drinks. This was a situation she never thought she would find herself experiencing.

On one visit she told me that she was so tired. When I inquired as to why, she told me that she had been packing and unpacking boxes all night. She just couldn't believe all she had to go through. She was just exhausted.

Very gently I asked her what boxes she was going through, she looked around and her empty room and smiling she said, "It must have all been in my mind, but this dying is hard work."

She let me know that you must look through all the things that you did, and all the things that others "did to you", and the hardest thing of all was forgiving yourself. You must forgive yourself for what you should have done but did not, as well as for the things that you did to others that were possibly not the kindest things. She explained that she had to repack the boxes, but she was not able to repack certain ones until she forgave herself and was kind to herself.

Our society allows us to be kind to others, but it frowns on us being kind to ourselves. We have established rules and a hierarchy of acceptable things in society based around what "others" who influence us believe. We can forgive others, but we must earn forgiveness for ourselves by doing a penance for things that they do not agree with. You spanked your child and society today says you should only do time out or verbal rebuke so the officers in charge of Children's Welfare determines that you have broken the rules and must pay a punitive price that involves not seeing your children, not being able to reprimand them and so on.

As humans we then morph these lessons to everything that we do in life, always knowing that someone else knows better how to live our lives and what is good for us. We have developed an entire system of laws and rules to control what others do and what is acceptable in society. You break one of the rules and you are off to jail to do a punishment that we, as society, has also developed as penance.

On another level this is referred to as atonement both in Biblical and philosophical arenas. Many other practices and belief systems speak of atoning for the things that we did in our life. Everything from Hinduism and modern-day spiritual beliefs to Judeo Christian belief systems have a form of atonement. Some refer to it as getting right with God, making your peace with others and so on. It appears that the hardest, and most often the last lesson that we learn is to love ourselves as we love others.

Those with whom I was assisting would explain what they are doing in terms we could understand, such as going through boxes, unpacking, and repacking, looking at all things that needed review from their earthly experience. They wanted to make sure that we understood all aspects of this journey.

They were often surprised when I asked them how

they could have done something physical, such as going through boxes. An example is Bethel who looked around and chuckled because she experienced the mental gymnastics of going through these "boxes" as real during this time but knew there were no boxes in her room and in no way could she have physically gone through them.

They would smile and tell me that it was in their mind, but they are still tired from doing that all night! One bit of advice that they gave me was to forgive and ask for forgiveness while you can still enjoy and benefit from it, don't wait till the end of life because you don't get to bask in the warmth of forgiving for very long before you leave. Energy is spent keeping the anger and frustration going for long periods and that energy could be used to do other things and learn other lessons.

Forgiveness does not require the other person to accept it, it requires us to offer it and accept the fact that it is over, and in the past, so we can move forward. All energy is spent on forward movement at this time of life and the requirement is for mental energy, not physical mobility.

The limited energy that we possess at this point in our lives should not be spent maintaining anger, frustration or hatred towards others. It should be focused on accepting and learning to love those who are in our life's circle as the beings that they are.

5
PROCESSING AND THE JOURNEY

To those who are watching there is a playbook.
Things will happen as they should.

PROCESSING AND THE JOURNEY

While I know that all journeys are different, what caught my attention was the fact that the process was the same and the transition was very methodical both physically, mentally, and spiritually. The body does a very methodical shutdown which is difficult to accept as a living, healthy person. Our mindset is to maintain the physical body and to do that you must eat and drink to live.

Nature provides us with reflexes and innate knowledge that we must replenish the energy that we expend daily, but it also knows that at end of life we no longer need these things. It is difficult to understand that the body just cannot continue, it is too physically impaired.

Many frustrated family members would tell the loved one "you will die if you don't eat." What they did not understand is that their loved one is dying, so they do not need to eat. The body has all the fuel it needs, and eating will only require an already paused digestive system to store food it does not need.

The appetite declines, they sleep more, and have very vivid dreams and they can recount them accurately. They talk to others you cannot see and will often reach for things that "aren't there". Those who chose not to understand convince themselves that the loved one is hallucinating, and it is the medications that they are being given that causes them to do these things. At any point in life if you are taking pain medications because they are needed you will "use them" and they will not cause hallucinations. Those who are abusing drugs will hallucinate because they do not need the medication and their body is trying to use and rid the body of these medications because it does not know what to do with them.

After a time, they slow their liquid intake, and they are no longer hungry or thirsty. The body processes shut down the same way, the digestion slows, until they stop eating and drinking completely. This is more difficult on the others that they are leaving behind than it is to the person leaving the earthly world.

One of the more difficult things to explain to the family or caregivers is that they no longer need to eat or drink. That the transition will be more difficult if they force them to eat, even a small amount, because the body is no longer needing or able to process food. Initially they may try to eat to please the caregiver but eventually they will simply set the food aside and not make any attempt to eat or drink. They are not trying to upset anyone, but it will only make them more uncomfortable during the end-of-life process.

One fear that is most frequently expressed is **"*what***

does it feel like to not take the last breath, won't I feel like I am suffocating?" A simple "no" does not cut it at this point. This is a very real fear because we have all held our breaths until we were forced to take a breath. We have all seen shows that demonstrate the exaggerated gyrations of the body when someone is being physically strangled and how awful that appears to be as the person struggles to breathe.

The body's processing deals with this concern by the individuals' breathing slowing gradually. They will normally breathe a few minutes, then miss a few breaths, breathe again, miss some breaths, and this will continue until there are longer spaces between breaths and eventually, they no longer breath. This can start several days before the final transition and as a caregiver you will find yourself taking breaths for them. It is a very unconscious action and will not bother them in the least. It is important to relax and work with the individual where they are in the process because they need support and not someone that is afraid because their breathing is irregular. Even in everyday life we have fluctuations in our breathing depending on the level of activity, focus we are using to accomplish a task and so on.

Spiritually and religiously, there are many ideas on when the actual death occurs and when the spirit is separated from the physical world. It is generally agreed that the body is the vessel for the soul or spirit and that the body requires the spirit and not the spirit needing the body.

You can argue this from many perspectives, but the primary belief is that the spirit, the energy that the body needs to function, leaves the body and then the body dies. You are not in the body when that last breath should occur. You never experience what that would feel like to suffocate, and you do not struggle for that last breath because you do not need it. This is important because those observing need to realize the peace that those transitioning experience.

THE SPIRIT LEAVES THEN THE BODY DIES.

Many of the people that I worked with spoke to me about transitioning between both worlds several times before they made the final transition. It can occur several times before the final transition and they can recall vividly what they are doing and who is with them.

At times they get very confused and cannot understand why that person they were just talking to has left, they are no longer here. Where did they go? It is interesting because they know the entities and the "names" of those who are with them and they describe them as they would have seen them in this physical world, but they do not understand when I would ask them if they just knew them and they were a spot of light type energy or if they were solid and like our human forms just in a different dimension. They would tell me "it was my dad, or it was Uncle Louie" etc. but not if it was an image or just an energy. Too much detail I assume!

They can interact on both sides of the veil and they may get confused about why you are in Heaven with them because you were not transitioning. They may ask why you are here or a question about where they are and where did their loved one go that has transitioned that they had just met.

Be kind but honest with them and explain to them that this is one of the only times in life that they get to experience both sides. They see the family who are living, and they are also able to experience all the family and friends that have transitioned.

This is the time when you can ask the best questions and get the explanation of what is occurring to them during the process. Bethel would talk to me about "dream dancing with her father". He passed when she was 14 years of age and she is now in her 80's, and she was so excited about the things that they would do together as this process unfolded. He came multiple times during her transitioning process, and she was always pleased and very calm when he had been to see her.

The interesting thing is that they all speak of going to Heaven and they meet with others that had crossed over, but they do so in the tense that "they" the spirit had come to see "them" the transitioning person. They are able to interact and do things that we would do in this physical realm. No one could tell me exactly how they would do things, but they always described it as how we in the physical realm would do things.

At one point, Bethel spoke to me about a dream that she had and there were two adults and two children that kept making themselves known to her. She was very agitated by their presence and when I asked her about what they wanted she said she didn't know. I suggested to her that maybe she could ask them what they wanted and why they were here to see her.

Bethel did exactly that when they came again. They were able to tell her that they "just wanted to make sure she had what she needed, and they would help her in any way they could as the process continued." They were there to encourage her. She also asked them who they were, and they informed her that "they were her cousin, spouse and two children who had passed during the great depression." This was my first understanding that others you may never have met in this life, who had lived during a different physical time frame, but are spiritually connected to you, will come back, and help you as you transition. There are no time frames in the next level, and it appears that you can move freely among people and situations.

This shows that time frames are different and not as we experience them. Many laws of physics appear to be proven as we go through the transitioning process. The Law of Time distinguishes between the universal time that has a natural order and the artificial time upon which we base our daily lives allowing us some control over the world as we perceive it. The Law of Time is based on universal Synchronicity that allows for everything to be based in the natural based universe.

6
END OF LIFE PROCESSES

Consensus is:

"If you wonder if todays the day, its not the day. You will always know the day and time that you are going to pass."

WHAT DOES THE BODY EXPERIENCE AT THE END OF LIFE?

There are some very specific things that you can look for physically to know when the end of life, as we know it, occurs. Breathing stops, heart stops, muscles relax, those are the simple things that occur.

One thing that you will notice is the sense of peace and relaxation that envelops the person. They may be in pain, but the medical community usually can keep that controlled with medications. There is nothing in the pain control that will speed the death because they need those medications to control their pain.

Families have reported to me that it was the morphine that "killed" their loved one. My response is that it was the disease and end of life transitioning that took their loved one and the morphine simply allowed that transition with less pain thus making it easier for them to transition. Those medications are not what is causing your loved one to **see** and talk to others that you cannot see, it is part of the transitioning process.

They may have very active situations where they reach for things that others can't see or they may have no attempts to reach out physically, but they are active mentally in this process. All the things that you are observing are a result of a very active mental process that the physical body is responding to.

There are different phases that we should look for when working with those who are transitioning. It is important to recognize the changes that are occurring. They physically relax, the body sends out the signals to slow the daily processes and they are open to talking if they have the physical energy to do so.

Talking is something that requires a great deal of physical energy, not only to speak but to process the thoughts and the answers to questions. While we are living, we can notice how tired we get after a long day of interacting with others, and we are even more tired when trying to explain things that are new to others so that they can understand.

I always ask the person that is in the process of transitioning "who is with us in the room." Initially I explain to them that they will begin seeing others who have crossed over and that there is nothing to be afraid of because they will not hurt or harm us. When they tell me that someone specific is here, I always ask them if they are afraid or think that person might harm them. They rarely think that they will harm them and are happy to see them. These energies are there to assist the person across to the next level of existence. You may learn more about this person than even their family knew about their life.

My mother passed recently and due to COVID-19 we were not allowed in during her transitioning until the very last minutes that she had left on earth. Fortunately, she had a nurse that was astute and asked questions that we would have asked had we been allowed in. The final conversation went like this, "Donna you seem to be staring at that point in the wall, what are you seeing?" My mother replied, "its Daddy and Mom and the Baby". She then passed peacefully. Her voice got very excited when she saw the Baby. We did not know that she had a baby that had not lived but I always wondered why my oldest sister and I were a year apart, there was 3 years between me and my next younger sister and then she and my two younger brothers were also stair steps apart. My best guess is that she lost a baby between myself and my younger sister. This is a guess, but it allows me to explain the large gap in birthdays. People did not talk about the loss of a baby as significant as they do now. You were to put it away and move forward.

It is important to write things down for the other members who are not able to be present during the transitioning. The individual will provide me the names and how they fit into their "Veil side" life. I always write things for the family because they can then reflect and share with the others in the family and gain a sense of peace related to the passing. You must always be aware of the secrets that others may share with you do to the normal filters not being in place.

One man that I was working with gave me a phone number and asked me to contact his son. There were several children already present and I asked why he had not been called. He told me that this was a son that his wife did not know about. He said he did not want the son to come visit but he did want him to know.

This put me in a difficult position because I was asked to keep a secret from his wife and other children. He felt he had protected this secret all through his life and wanted to maintain that secret. I took the number and told him I would let him know.

I went into the kitchen area to talk to the family after we finished. His wife calmly informed me that the man's other son had been contacted and he would be coming for a visit. I was surprised but she told me she had always known about this son but had used that knowledge to her advantage during the marriage. I did not inquire any further because this was a marital issue and end-of-life is not a time to work on manipulations, but I was very aware that he would be working on atonement and it would be much easier since this lifelong secret was now in the open on both sides.

When working with a person who is in the process of transitioning you can see when the person's energy has left the body. When the energy that is the spirit leaves, a look of peace shows on the face. Another time to be alert is when they experience seeing God. At that point there is absolutely a glow that comes over the person. It is amazing and experienced by only a few guests that are accompanying the person on their end of life journey. This is not something that is restricted to only a certain few that are allowed to see, it is because we never know when it will occur during the journey so it may be a time when no one is sitting with them or specifically watching them. Those who are privileged enough to have observed it all report that it is the most amazing earthly thing they have ever seen.

7
NO ONE TRANSITIONS FROM THIS LIFE TO THE NEXT ALONE

THOSE WHO HAVE GONE BEFORE WILL ASSIST WITH MY TRANSITION

No one transitions from this life to the next level alone. This is the only time that you can see both sides of the life that we all share. Others will come to you that have transitioned already and you are able to interact with them on their plane, just as you are able to interact with those physical people on this side of the veil.

People have asked me, and suggested, that I talk to the dead. I do not. I listen to what the person who is transitioning is sharing with me. They will call others by a pet name, may have a specific reason for what is happening and will share activities that others are doing that we can't see. They may talk to me about others that I have not heard the family speak of previously but when I share the event with the family, they usually can identify that person.

Often those transitioning want to introduce me to the spirits that are there with us during this phase of life. I gently explain to them that I am unable to meet them at this tie but as soon as I am able, I would be happy to meet them. They are usually very surprised that I can't see the others, but I explain to them that end of life or transitioning is the only time that we can actually see both sides of the of the veil. I encourage them to take advantage and enjoy this experience and not allow anyone to tell them that they are not experiencing what is clearly occurring.

I found that it was a great comfort to the family if I wrote the things down that the individual was telling me rather than just pass the information along orally. They were able to identify the people in the transitioners "dreams" and usually were able to identify why a certain date was important. It may take some time but often as they were cleaning out the individuals' personal items, they would come across items that explained many of the things that the individual was speaking about.

What I do is to listen to those around me, pick up on energy and talk to those who are able to share their experiences as they transition. I have been referred to by many names and have been given much personal information that others shared as they are transitioning.

I have gained a huge respect for those who are going through this process and the peace that most of them feel as they transition. Fear that may be present at the beginning of the transition changes to acceptance and understanding as they progress and arrive at the end of the journey.

They are also continuing to deal with family

members and loved ones that continue to encourage them to live, to fight the end of this life and they are continually tearful when they are near them. It is important for you, as a caregiver, to provide them with support and reassurance. You are grieving and they understand that, but they also want you to be excited and interested in what their next journey will unwrap. This evolution is so amazing that it is something that we all should encourage and support.

No one that I spoke with during the transition wanted to cause emotional pain to their loved ones but they also understood that they needed to have their support so they could move on comfortably. If you are not comfortable with this process and what they want to share with you, they will not share the information. They will still go through the process, but they will simply keep things to themselves.

Imagine the comfort and peace that you will feel when your loved one is able to share with you who is with them during this process. During this time, they are able to share that Mom is there with them, or they are back with their family that have already crossed over. They want to share the joy that seeing them has provided and also the fact that they appear to be doing fine. This is a new experience for them and they are excited to share all of it with others. What they do not have is the energy to deal with negative or doubting people that will not join in their joy.

JENNY

One family that I was working with when I first began writing the information for had a mother that was passing, Jenny had been married several years and her husband had been gone about 10 years. She also had a daughter that had passed when she was five years old. I did not know this at the time but it became apparent quickly.

Jenny would talk to me but she would look past me and talk to someone behind me. She would scold that person and tell them to "sit down and be still". She repeated this several times and I asked her who she was talking to, she told me that "it was Uncle Louie."

I left a note for the daughters and they called and let me know that everyone called their dad Uncle Louie, even their mom called him that.

Jenny told me on one visit that she had been spending time with others. I asked her who and she spoke of a young girl who had been swinging and beckoned her over. She was so excited that she got to see her. She did not tell me the girls name because we moved on to a different topic at that point.

When talking to the daughters again they told me that Jenny had a daughter that had passed. Much of the time spent with Jenny it appeared that I was a bystander that was allowed to step into her experiences, but she didn't feel the need to keep me informed as to what was going on. She did not explain things, but she allowed me to "visualize" what was occurring almost as an invisible piece of equipment in the room. She would talk around me as though I was just something in her line of sight. I was able to write for the daughters all of the things that were going on, many of the things they were not aware of because they occurred prior to their births. The first daughter passed before either of them were born and many of the activities centered around her life at that time.

During one of the daughters visits Jenny informed them that she was all packed and ready to leave on her trip. They asked her if that was coming soon and she told them it would be "tonight". She passed very peacefully that night with both daughters at her side. They were so happy to know that their father and their sister that they had never known were in Heaven with her.

LET US START WITH THE BASICS:

It is important to provide you with a basic starting point so that we can speak the same language as you begin to understand the process of transitioning. Who wants to be called out by someone who is passing because we don't understand what is going on?!

They have their own language, their own perspective and their own idea of how things should and will go. The last thing we can choose in life is who is with us when we pass. I have seen families not leave the side of the loved one until they all need to go to the bathroom at the same time. The minute they leave the room their loved one transitions, and they are shocked. Your loved one will do what they feel that **you** can handle, if they don't want you to remember them as they are taking that last breath they will pass when you are out of the room so you won't see that. Likewise, I have seen individuals hang on for weeks as they wait for a loved one to get there, so they can see them one last time before they transition. Shortly after that person arrives, they peacefully transition to the other side of the veil.

You will see as we take this journey how things happen and how they are truly in the control of the individual who is transitioning. You will have a better understanding and peace related to the end of life and the beginning of the next level of existence.

Understanding is essential so we can see the life of the person transitioning through what they share with us. They will share information if we don't show fear of the information. They don't ever want to frighten us and will withhold information if they think that you are not able to understand or accept what they are going to share. So many things happen in a lifetime that it is difficult for us to remember; and we may not have been around when many of them occurred to others. Such things include birth of a child, marriage, courting etc. These are things we did not see especially If we are the child of this person. We may have some faint knowledge, but I suggest that they talk to their aunts and uncles and other siblings to get a better understanding of what they are trying to share.

At times it seems to be a code, but if you listen and ask questions you can figure it out. Individuals have told me the day and time that they are going to pass; I began to share that information with families, so they can be with them and be prepared and accept the reality of what is happening.

One family asked why I was able to get that information and they were not. It is very simple; I am there to listen and let them know what was happening; they are already grieving and may be overwhelmed. The loved ones were processing all the physical world things that are on this side of the Veil, those transitioning shared with me what was on the other side of the Veil.

Verbiage: This is the very basic part of the process. I learned it over time, and it is essential to understand where the individual is in the process. As we go through our lives we talk about end of life as Death, Dying, Dead etc. We have our words that we use on this side of the "Veil" and as the individual gets closer to transitioning, they begin to use different words. Their language transitions to crossing over, passing on, moving on and transitioning. It is never an ending type word that we would use but it is a word that provides that understanding that they are moving on to the next level, they are passing on and transitioning. They gain the understanding that it is simply a changing of form.

End of life is the process of the spirit, the energy that provides the physical body with the ability to function, moves into a different form. The mainstay of physics is that energy is neither created nor destroyed, it simply changes form. The Bible refers to that human energy as the spirit. This spirit is released as the body no longer requires it, and then the body dies or stops functioning.

It is important to understand that the spirit leaves then the body dies. There are many reasons that this is important and as I relay the stories and the beauty of the passing, and you will come to an understanding of this process.

Purpose of life is the teaching and learning of lessons. When those lessons have been learned and we have taught others what we were here to teach we are able to move on and transition to the next level. It is important that when working with others we listen to what they say they "need" as they get ready to transition.

They are often able to identify what is missing and we may be able to assist. It may be seeing someone they have been angry with, someone not seen in years, someone that they want to apologize to or just acknowledge their importance. When that is completed, either in person or spiritually, the individual will be able to transition peacefully.

No one has the same lessons to learn or teach. I have yet to determine from those who are transitioning if the lessons are predetermined in heaven so it guides our future in this life, or if the lessons that are required of all of us in this life are not predetermined and we are to learn any lesson presented. Could it be possible that we are all sent to learn love, empathy, compassion and each life teaches it differently, but the lesson is still learned?

We are so busy in our society we overlook what it is we need to look at or work on, but if you are still and listen to what is tugging at your heart you will learn what these things may be. It may be patience, understanding, kindness, or even being firmer with others to speak your truth.

Spiritual Energy is the energy that is the driving

force behind our lives. It can be positive or negative and we all chose how we work with this energy. Nothing comes into our lives without a purpose and it can work for or against us as we move forward. I have worked with hundreds of individuals that have transitioned and there were only three that I can truly identify as being negative and literally looking at Hell as they passed. They fought the transition and begged for others to help them. It was very frightening even to myself at times and I instinctively knew that I must leave after offering them the options that I had available.

They refused those options and we both knew that they had made their choice. I learned that the choice is always the individuals, no one else can force them into accepting or declining the things that are before them. You see where you are going and what energy force you will be transitioning toward. You have till the last minute to change your heart and accept what is offered but you always have free choice to make that decision, good or bad.

Something that I found interesting was that those who appeared to be looking at very negative consequences were comfortable talking to me as this transitioning process occurred, but if I physically touched them, they would recoil in pain or scream a blood curdling scream until I moved my hand. One lady that I worked with had been with Hospice about a year. Every visit she would say "I'm dying" and I would say "you are but not today". She came on hospice early in the process and refused to get out of bed to speak with me. She was perfectly capable of getting up but a control method with others that she used was to refuse to get up so they would leave. When she told me she would not get up I said that was fine I would just get on the bed and talk to her there. It was a huge bed. She tried other things to get me to leave like not looking at me, closing her eyes etc. but something kept pulling me back there to see her every week. It was an interesting exchange, and we had many delightful discussions. As she was finally transitioning, they moved her into a quiet dark room with a much smaller bed. During our final meeting she would reach for my hand and the minute we touch she would let out a blood curdling scream. I pulled my hand back and she stopped. She reached for my hand two more times and again let out the scream. When I removed my hand she stopped again. She would resume talking as though nothing had happened. After the third series of screams I told her that there appeared to be something that she needed to complete and that she knew what she needed to do. She looked at me and very matter of factly said "no". At this time, I know that I had done all that I could do and told her I needed to leave.

    I will be honest with you this completely freaked

me out! In all my experience I had never had this happen before nor since. I personally believe that she knew she must accept Christ, but she chose not to do that. This was her personal choice and Biblically to move into Heaven you must accept Christ as the Son of God. This was her belief system; she attended the Methodist Church her entire life but in the final transition phase she refused to acknowledge Christ. She was very antagonist to the beliefs she had been raised in through the Church. Her belief system was that there was a Heaven and Hell so if she refused to acknowledge the very things required to go to Heaven then Hell was the other option.

The interesting thing was that it was a ten minute, drive back to my office. When I got there, I went in to talk to my supervisor to let her know that this was really disturbing, and I would prefer not to return. She told me that I did not have to go back because the family had called, and it had upset them also. They were not in the room with us, but they would here her scream and it was unnerving to them.

Those who were not looking at the negative consequences were never in pain or upset when I touched them. In fact they would asked to be touched almost as an anchor to this side of the Veil.

Basic process of transitioning begins with the individual seeing or hearing little children that others cannot see or hear. They may ask you to watch them play or ask you to tell them to be quiet because they are too loud.

Many will see others that we cannot see, talk to people that are not here on this side of the Veil and tell you about things that they should have completed, or that they did finish a particular act. This participation may be a purely mental process, but they are still exhausted or exhilarated!

Many will have "dreams" of others, that they may never have met in their lifetime, but that energy has been there to see them. They will describe them as they were in this life and when I asked why they are presented this way it was gently explained to me that this is the only way that they could understand. They always have a purpose and provide explanation when asked what is happening and why that entity was here to see them.

After they begin to see others the natural process is that they will begin to slow their eating. The family often encourages them to eat even after it is explained to them that the body very methodically shuts down. It is a very deliberate process and the body is no longer able to digest food. They don't need it because they are transitioning. As the body becomes weaker, family members assume that they are hallucinating because their interactions with the next level become more active and interactive. They may have very active times where they are reaching for things and trying to do things, but it is one sided, only because we can't see what is happening beyond the Veil.

They always keep their sense of humor and will tell you whatever you want to know if you remember to ask. Always remember to ask because they may be open to you a side of yourself that you hadn't recognized. I am always learning of different things that occur as I speak with others.

The "side" of yourself that you may discover is a spiritual side that others recognize in you and are able to see. We often are too busy in this realm to notice that we have been provided gifts that we use throughout our lives but do not acknowledge because we are too busy chasing the issues of this life. These gifts may also frighten us because we have not taken the time to investigate them.

Learning to listen to those at end of life was a gift that I could not walk away from because I felt that it was my moral responsibility to help this level of transitioning individual. They were telling their final story and others wanted to know what it was but did not understand how to listen.

There are a few questions that I wished I had thought to ask and there are no repeats in this situation. I wish I had asked my client what name she knew me by when she stated that Pam was not the name she knew me by. She passed before I could ask, but I am glad that I finally got there so she could pass peacefully.

The other question was when I was sitting with an individual and I asked her who was with us, she said that her mother and father were in the room. She wanted me to meet them, but I told her I would when I could, but it was not possible right now.

Her husband had passed about 20 years prior and when I asked her where he was, she told me "he was busy right now but would be coming later to take her home." I should have asked "what was he doing." I will not get that opportunity again and I regret not asking.

Closer to the final hours the individual may quit talking or they may appear to have multiple things going on at the same time. You will see multiple changes in their facial expressions as they have conversations and deal with their life. They may wake occasionally for short periods or sleep straight through at that point. They are very busy, and their mind is going constantly.

Another thing that will occur is the individual will have periods of breathing normally, then they may miss a breath or two. It is very natural for those taking care of them to try to breath for them. You will find yourself taking a loud deep breath as though they can hear you and will start breathing again. This variation in breathing pattern can go on for a few days before the individual transitions. They may also have "the death rattle". That is caused by mucus settling in the throat that the person is unable to cough out. If it becomes a problem the Nursing staff will be able to provide them with something that will assist in drying this so it is no longer a problem.

8
"IN THE BEGINNING ….."

THE BEGINNING

As I begin to write the story of the individuals that I have been with throughout their journey in this life and their transitions to the next life it is important to understand that I am not someone that speaks with the dead, I do not "see" dead people and I do not make any attempt to speak with the "other side". Everything that I report I saw and heard from this side of life.

I started my journey working in a Hospice program in Illinois. I showed up as a new Social Worker wondering what in the world possessed me to take a job working in Hospice! I did not know anything about death and dying and I was terrified at the prospect of being with someone who was dealing with the end of life. My employer assumed I had a clue about what my job entailed, and I went on the internet about what a Hospice Social Worker was to do. The internet told me I was to make sure they had a burial plot, a funeral home, insurance and so on. That did not seem to require much but surely there was more to dying than just making sure they had a place to be buried. How could life come down to just that odd detail?

I was looking through the paperwork that I was to complete and there were no clues in there either. As I took on my first patient, I met a person that I will call Bethel. She was alert, oriented, and had a very infectious laugh, with many friends that would come by all the time. From these friends I learned about her life and the things that she did not speak of often. They found her to be the most gracious and giving person that they had ever met. She was always there to assist even though she had lived a very difficult life herself.

It is important to know that Bethel was on Hospice for an extended period of time. She had a slow decline and was alert and oriented throughout most of it. She was able to talk to me until the last hours of her life. Most of her life she lived hand to mouth but was generous with others.

Bethel's father had passed when she was 14 years of age. She raised herself with her close family but did not speak of that until she was closer to transitioning. She worked as a personal aid until she was no longer able to work. She was ill, but I was able to build a relationship with her and she promised to tell me everything that was happening as she went through this end-of-life process.

She told me often of "dream dancing with her father" and "horseback riding with her father". She often reported interacting with him and would look very peaceful when talking of him. I asked her at one point if she was there or if this was a dream and she told me it seemed like a dream, but he was here with her. She was so excited about seeing him.

On one visit Bethel told me of a group of people that had come to see her. She was very agitated and wanted me to explain who they were and what they wanted. She said that they had come several times and she did not know what they wanted.

When talking to her she did not recognize them, and they did not come close enough for her to speak with them. I encouraged her to ask them who they were and what they wanted. She agreed to do that and thought they may leave her alone at that time.

After they visited about 3 times, she was able to tell me that these were her cousins and their children who crossed over during the depression. She was very comfortable again and when I asked her what they wanted she was able to tell me that they just wanted to let her know that they were here if she needed anything in the process of crossing over.

She never spoke about them again as she moved on to other parts of the transitioning process.

During one visit she was telling me that she was so exhausted. She had been bedfast for weeks and never got up for any reason, but she told me about moving all the things around and going through all the boxes full of the events of her life. Every box had something else in it and as she viewed the event she couldn't move it to a different box to be repacked until she either forgave the person involved in that activity or forgave herself for what had happened. She explained that the most difficult thing she had to do was forgive herself. It was easy to forgive others.

She decided this must be what others always explained as atonement. She stated very matter of factly, that you either atone while you are alive and you get it over with and forgive yourself for things or you do it as you are crossing over, but you have to do it.

Bethel explained that as you work through this transitioning process you can see why all the bad things in life happen so that all the good things can follow. It was a huge tapestry, and it was beautiful. Everything made sense at this point.

Several times she clearly pointed out that you either work through these issues as you go through life or you work through them as you are transitioning. Bethel felt that given this knowledge, you should work through them during your life and forgive others and forgive yourself. She told me that this is really hard work and takes a lot of energy.

As she progressed through the end of life, she was very ill with bedsores and in a great deal of pain. I asked her why she was still here, and she explained to me that they told her it was not her time, and she could not cross over one minute before it was her time. I boldly asked who "they" were and just got a look that spoke volumes of "how could you possibly not know who they are?". I did not ask that question again but made the assumptions that it was all those she was meeting during this transitioning process who were already on the other side of the Veil.

On the next visit I sat next to her for a period. I did not touch her because I didn't want to wake or disturb her due to the level of pain I knew she was experiencing. After a few minutes she opened her eyes and asked me why I had not touched her. I told her I did not want to disturb her, she smiled. She told me that any time I came to see her, I was always to touch her and hold her hand; she said I had the calmest soul she had ever felt.

This taught me that we are all energy, it is felt by others as we work and interact with them going through life. We can be a positive influence on others, or we can carry negativity with us and make others frustrated and upset when they deal with us. In life our journey should be based on providing positive energy to others and allowing them to grow and develop as they move forward.

After being with Bethel through her journey I had a better understanding of what happens but still did not know what my role was, but I knew this was the field I was meant to work in. I wanted to bring about any peace and understanding that I could not only to those who were transitioning but also to the families. This is a time of life that we don't talk about as a society, it is different from what we focus on daily and it is very institutionalized. We think that it happens quickly, that someone is there and then gone.

Lessons from Bethel include: *that we do have to forgive ourselves, that is the most difficult, but we must work through things.

- We do have atonement for our acts both good and bad.
- We have an energy that others feel, and we can choose how we present this energy. We can be calm, anxious, angry but whatever that energy is we pass that to others, and they are able to pick up on that energy and react accordingly.
- Time is a relative thing. She had family coming from the great depression and this was the 2000's. Energy is always there
- We can speak to both sides of the Veil at this time in our lives. Those who are living and those who passed over.
- We will not pass one minute before our time

During my career with Hospice, I would work with several people at the same time. I frequently made 4-5 visits daily to different people to assist them and their families with the process of transitioning. At times funny things would happen and many people thought that their loved one did not realize that they were dying.

One family was in Illinois and when I arrived at the home the wife pulled me aside and told me that they had not told her husband that he was on Hospice or that he was dying. I told her that I would not lie to him, but I also would not just flat out present it to him. I reassured her that I was pretty sure he realized what was happening and he was aware that he was at end of life.

After a conversation in the kitchen about what this process entailed and updating the family on what they could expect as he drew closer to transitioning, I went into the living room area to meet the client.

As I walked in to meet him, he stood up, stretched out his had and informed me his name was Bob, he had life insurance in place, had a pre-paid funeral plan at Johnson funeral home and he also had his plot purchased and the headstone picked out. I took his hand and shook it and looked at the wife and mouthed "I think he knows". She was shocked because she had worked so hard to "protect" him. The lesson here is that people know, we can work and try to hide things but end of life is something that we will always know.

The theory is as follows, "if you wake up and wonder if today is the day, it is not. You will always know when it is the day. Family can try to ignore the signs and try to convince you that it is not the beginning of the transitioning but the person that is transitioning will always know.

JILL

Another client that I worked with, we will call her Jill, was a person that was very well cared for in her home. She was anxious to learn about the dying process and what it entailed. She would ask questions and would insist that her daughter sit in with us so she would also understand what she was going through.

Finances were limited and Hospice provided a great deal of support where they could, to provide her with everything that she needed. Her daughter was her primary caregiver and assisted in all areas of her care. This daughter trusted others and would often leave her siblings with her mother when she ran out for groceries or to run errands.

Jill was very verbal and very religious, but she always wanted to make sure that everyone knew she was not going to allow this process to be colored by her religion, she was going to see it for exactly what it was.

Jill was bedfast which made her care a bit more difficult due to her inability to assist with moving and repositioning. She was asking me when certain people will be here to see her, I suggested that they would come when it was closer to her time to cross over. She would "humpf" and we would go to the next subject!

As Jill got more ill, she was seeing children playing outside her window. She asked me to go out and ask their names and I was able to redirect her by asking what difference it would make if she knew their names. She just smiled and stated, "that's a nice way to say they are not there"- She caught me!

Next visit she was complaining that they were in the house making too much noise and they were going to wake her husband (he had passed several years before). I talked to her frequently about what was happening, and she told me what was happening to her.

She told me that she had been in Heaven. She said, "it was beautiful" and when I asked, "what did it look like", she told me "she couldn't tell me". When I asked, "am I not supposed to know because I was not at that point in life?", she told me "no", it was because we don't have words to describe how beautiful it is."

I had spoken with the daughter and explained to her what it may appear to look like when her mother experiences God. I explained that she will glow like an angel and that she will get an all-encompassing expression of peace and that expression will remain with her until the end occurs. I explained that this often occurs with no one else around so she should not be upset if she does not see it, it does not mean that it did not occur.

Her daughter was so excited when I saw her next. She was in the room when her mother met God, and she was amazed that her mother truly glowed. It was a learning process for the daughter since she was trying to resolve her agnostic belief system with what she was witnessing.

Jill constantly told her daughter to make sure she read all the books in the reading room before she gave them away. She was insistent on this until her passing.

During the funeral, another daughter had brought a U Haul to the house and loaded up all the antiques and furniture and left the daughter that had provided all the care to their mother with only the essentials.

Several months later the daughter contacted me to tell me that as she was going through the reading room magazines and books as her mother requested. She found money between the pages of all the books. She was so relieved because her mother had tried to pass that information on before she transitioned, but as she grieved, she was slow to process what she had tried to tell her.

Lessons from Jill include:

- we begin this journey by seeing children who may also be of the spiritual world
- We do see God as we transition
- Even in our spiritual state we are able to see the beautiful energy that will allow us to glow in His presence.
- We keep our sense of humor and insight
- We understand and work to pass on information to our family and they must listen as we try to leave the tip and clues

I saw patients in all situations of life. Some had family doting on their every request and other had no family support. There were many reasons some individuals did not have one on one family support. It may be that the family needed to work, and employers would not give them time off to sit with a dying loved one, or it may be distance, or the other family members may be aging themselves and not physically able to provide the hours or intensity of the support that was needed.

Many in Hospice are in their 90's which means that their children may be in their early 70's and are not able to be with them. They are dealing with their own health issues and transportation issues. I would have staff tell me to get the family in here because their loved one is dying. It took training at each facility to bring them up to speed that they may not choose to be missing but may not have other options because of their own issues.

JACK

One man that I worked with was alone. He had no family close and he was getting ready to transition.

The family had wanted to transfer him to someplace closer to them in Pennsylvania, but time ran out. He had always been a rebel and lived his life alone and went his own way.

When I spoke with the family, they told me that Jack had moved away from everyone in his 30's and had no contact with the family for a long period. After he got sick and was in the nursing home, they started to look for his family with his permission. They used the limited information that they had and found his family. They wanted to have him back in their lives if even for a small amount of time.

When I would see him, he always talked about golfing and riding the train. There was nothing in his room to give any clues about his life so I would sit quietly with him and just talk about random things that would come up.

On one visit he was telling me that someone he did not know had been to see him. When I questioned him, he decided they were not in this world. It must have been someone not alive any longer because he never remembered this person in his travels.

I explained to him that no one passes from this world alone and others would come over and assist them across. He laughed slightly and looked up at the ceiling and said, "like all those people that just keep passing through here?" He asked why they do not stop; it was like a big parade of people just walking through. I was able to reassure him that when it was time they would stop and take him along with them. He may not recognize what they look like now, but he would be able to recognize their spirit as the time got closer. That reassured him because he was in awe of all the people passing through his room.

I had never had anyone say that before, usually it is people that they know even though they may not recognize them until they are closer to passing. My theory is that these may be people that he had interacted with during his lifetime, but that one special person is not able to come until the time is close.

I base that on my other experiences, but you can draw your own conclusions.

Do you ever feel like your life goes in circles and

you seem to have the same types of problems over and over again? It happens to all of us and I believe that it may be one of the lessons that we have not learned yet, we continue to make mistakes in response to that situation until we learn to speak for ourselves and as we learn one lesson, we can teach the other person involved the lesson that they need to learn in this life.

Often people do not know the past details of their loved one's life. One family that I was working with was very interested in assisting their grandmother in the process of passing, but they had limited information as to what her past held. We will call her Jessica.

JESSICA

Jessica had raised her three granddaughters because their mother had passed when they were small. Jessica was willing to take them on even though she would be a very non-traditional single parent. She had lost her husband before the girls were born so they knew very little about him or the marriage.

As Jessica became more involved, they were responsive to her every need. They made sure she was comfortable and had anything that she wanted. I had explained to them that she would be able to tell them when she was going to cross over and that she would not cross over alone.

Jessica began asking on a Thursday if it was Wednesday yet. They did not know why she was focused on Wednesday and brushed it off initially. I explained to them that at midnight on Wednesday they need to let her know. They promised that they would, and they carried through on that promise.

When I was there on Friday Jessica told me that there was a man at the foot of her bed. I asked if she was afraid of him or if she knew who he was and she said that she did not know who he was, but she was not afraid of him, in fact she stated that he was very funny. She described him tripping over the end of the bed and doing a pratfall!

On Sunday when I made a visit because Jessica was transitioning quickly and her granddaughters were young and a bit stressed, the man was at the middle part of the bed and still entertaining her. Again, she asked if it was Wednesday yet and I told her "no, not yet".

On my Tuesday visit she told me the man was at the head of the bed and he was dressed in a Tuxedo and he was very kind, she was drawn to him, but she was still not sure who he was, but she knew that she knew him. I spoke with the granddaughters and no one knew of any reason the Wednesday day was important to her, but they agreed to tell her when it was Wednesday.

They told her at 12:00 a.m. that it was Wednesday

and settled in beside her to assist as needed. Jessica passed at 3 a.m. with the family still not understanding why that day was important.

They called me a few weeks later as they were going through her things and they found her marriage license. Her 50th wedding anniversary would have been that very Wednesday that she transitioned. They were so pleased that she shared this journey with them even though they were unaware of the importance of that Wednesday date at the time.

Each journey is unique and based on our lives and the energy that we develop as we learn and teach our lessons.

Some journeys in transitioning are much more succinct and very clear what they are teaching.

JOHN

A gentleman that I will call John had been very angry at God for most of his adult life. His son had passed at the age of 12 in a tragic accident. John did not understand why his son died and no longer attended church after that accident. His wife was very concerned that he would not go to Heaven because of his anger and refusal to move past this hurt.

I had been to see him several times and it was obvious that he "tolerated" me because he thought he had to see me because I was with hospice. Trust me I never told anyone that they did not have to see me!

On one visit he was declining and was in a spare bedroom so his wife could sleep and he could keep the temperature cool as he preferred. While we were chatting, I asked him if I could bring him so flowers or something with color. He told me "yes" and I asked him what color he would prefer. He told me it did not matter because there were no colors in Heaven.

That surprised me and I asked why he thought there were no colors in Heaven, and he told me that it was all gold, silver, and pearl and it was beautiful. He told me that he had been there already and just came back because it was not his time yet and he could not go until it was his time. He said that he could not tell me what it was like because we had no way to describe it.

He was very much at peace and no longer angry at God. His wife was happy to know that he had finally moved past the anger that he had held his entire life. He spent a lot of energy being angry at God and he missed a lot of events and caused strife in his family due to that anger.

This is an extreme example of atonement. You forgive when you can or you carry that negative with you throughout your life, eventually you must forgive others and yourself for everything that occurs in this life.

MARY

One person that I was working with that was alone, due to the fact that she had begun her transition quickly and was transferred from her home to a hospital and now to a nursing home to die. I was sent to be with her during the transition as her daughter traveled in from Virginia trying to get there before her mother passed. While sitting in this very plain stark room I was able to be present for her as she transitioned. The oddest thing that I had ever experienced happened as she drew her last breath. The smell of roses became so strong in the room and while I looked everywhere in the room there was not a flower in sight. The facility nurse came in to check on her and let me know the update on the daughter and asked me where the roses were. She also smelled the very strong aroma of roses and was surprised when I told her there were no roses in the room. She walked out telling me that was weird!

When her daughter arrived I was able to share with her about the smell of roses. I told her I wished she had been early enough to smell them because it was amazing. She began to cry and shared with me that her mother was considered a "master gardener" and her specialty was roses.

To this day I have no clue how the smell of roses occurred and can only marvel at the strength of the spirit and what it can accomplish. That smell seemed to have come from every cell in her body, that is how strong it was at the time of transitioning!

People usually keep their sense of humor through out the process. I was working with a young woman who was battling breast cancer. She was very talkative and alert each time I saw her. On one of the final visits, she told me her brother had been there to see her and wanted her to go home with him. Of course, my mind went to the million questions of How will he take care of you? How is he going to get you home? Who will stay with you? The statement that I made was "I didn't know you had a brother". She informed me that he had crossed over when he was 25 from a motorcycle accident. She said they had a great visit and he would be back to take her home on Thursday.

I was very happy she wasn't leaving to go with her brother to finish her journey but I kept that to myself! Personally, she did not appear to me to be actively dying but I informed the staff that she was leaving on Thursday so they could be prepared.

When I returned to the facility to see her on Friday, I mentioned that she said she was leaving on Thursday. She laughed and said, "I am but not this Thursday"! While my professional opinion was that she was not close enough to transitioning yet I never second guess what the individual tells me. I guess I should have asked "which Thursday?" She was there a few more Thursday but she did pass on a Thursday, just as she told me she would.

You will know the day and time you are going to pass, if you wonder if today's the day, it is not.

ALICE

Another example of this is an individual that I was working with who was in her 80's. Her son was attentive but came at times when I was not in for a visit.

Alice and I were talking one afternoon, and she told me that her parents were there, and she wanted me to meet them. I explained to her that I was not able to meet them yet, but I would be happy to meet them when I was able. I asked her where her husband was, and she told me he was busy right then.

He had passed about 20 years ago. I asked her when he might get there to see her and she stated that he would be there at 6 p.m. I asked what she was going to do when he got here and she told me that she planned to leave with him and go home.

I called her son to let him know what she had told me. I explained to him that I was not telling him she was going to pass at 6:00, I was just telling him what she said, that his father was coming at 6:00 and she was planning to leave with him to go home.

He called me the next day and stated that he "so wanted to think I was just that crazy social worker". He was with his mother, she passed as the clock struck 6 p.m. and he says he knows that his dad was there to pick her up. He thanked me for telling him so he could be there with her as she transitioned.

It is important to share with others what those who are transitioning are telling us. You must be ready to be scoffed at, laughed at and generally discounted but if they pay attention to those passing, they will be able to put the pieces together themselves. They may never come to the point that they will admit that other energies are there with them, but they will be more comfortable with the transitioning of the loved one.

It is important to understand that our lives are so important, and we must look at what our situations and the learning and teaching that we can achieve. We experience that energies that have been with us in this life as we transition into the next level of learning and existence. Notice that each person knew those who came back to assist them across.

Do not be afraid to ask questions and to explore the unique things that occur in your lifetime. It is interesting and should be embraced. If you are experiencing something, more likely than not someone else will have a similar experience. Listen to your gut and follow your intuition. You may be excited about the places that it takes you. Our instincts as human beings bring us to an understanding of what this and the next life are waiting to show.

THOUGHTS FROM THE AUTHOR

Remember that nothing happens in this world be chance. All things are inter-related, and one will lead to another. Things will happen that you may not be able to explain but there is a purpose.

LEARN TO LAUGH AND LOVE AND ALWAYS FORGIVE THOSE AROUND YOU.

Forgiving does not mean forgetting if they have wronged you, it simply means that you will not carry anger or hatred forward. They suck energy from you that can be used to help others. Energy, as we have seen, can be positive and negative. Do not dwell or attempt to move into the negative energy. It may be something over your control level and may take you down a dark path.

The number one lesson that everyone should learn and take forward is ***do not be afraid to live.***

Everyone said that you will not pass one minute before it is your time. Death is a transition and not an end. We have a great deal of first-hand reports and information that shows it is not something to be feared but embraced and processed with others in our transitioning phase.

Call to Action

Go to the web sight for PKM Life Transitions to keep up to date with the Pod cast and the latest release dates for upcoming book.

www.pkmlifetranstions.net

Share your insights with loved ones and friends to bring this topic into the place of normal daily discussions. It is important that we talk about end-of-life so we can gain an understanding of what to expect and a comfort with living our lives to the fullest.

Sign up for my news letter by sending your email information to:

pkmlifetransitions2@gmail.com.

I would also be very interested in reading and learning about any occurrences that you have experienced as you go through life.

www.ingramcontent.com/pod-product-compliance
Lightning Source LLC
Chambersburg PA
CBHW060207050426
42446CB00013B/3013